MANIFESTING JOY
&
HAPPINESS DAILY

This book is dedicated
to you, the reader.
Some I know,
others I don't.
My wish is that the
book inspires you,
lifts you up,
and helps you shine
your light brighter.

MANIFESTING JOY
&
HAPPINESS DAILY

by Michael D. Jones

SILVERHEART PRODUCTIONS

ISBN 979-8-218-10599

INTRODUCTION

I wrote this book to help you get clear in order to manifest your dreams. You can make it a part of your daily ritual, write notes to inspire yourself, and take time to absorb the meaning of the words- to see what they reveal and how it fits into your life. This book is for **YOU**! Use it as a tool to channel positivity and bring in abundance. Let it be a reminder of who you are, and use it as a launching point on your journey to becoming the person you want to be: happy, whole, and living life to its full potential.

The last page is a tear-out sheet. Write your name in the center and hang it somewhere visible- a bathroom mirror, the front door, wherever you will see it. It's your daily reminder to be active in creating the life you want to live. NOW is the time for forward motion!

Steps for Setting Intentions:
BE CLEAR.
Be as specific as possible about what you're asking for from the Universe.

START SMALL.
Grow your confidence by setting small, achievable goals. Once you've accomplished the small stuff and started to gain momentum, keep building with bigger and bolder intentions. That way the Universe can reward you. Your imagination is the only limit!

LET GO.
Set an intention, say it out loud, concentrate on feeling it, and then LET IT GO. Let the Universe work for you.

PRACTICE GRATITUDE
Give thanks for all of the GOOD in your life, then feel more of that goodness coming in.

EVERY DAY
ABOVE GROUND
IS A GOOD DAY

BE GRATEFUL FOR
THE MOMENTS
THAT BROUGHT
YOU HERE

gratitude
noun: /ˈgradəˌt(y)o͞od/

the quality of being thankful; readiness to show appreciation for and to return kindness.

~Oxford English Dictionary

Being grateful today allows the UNIVERSE to reward you with ABUNDANCE tomorrow.

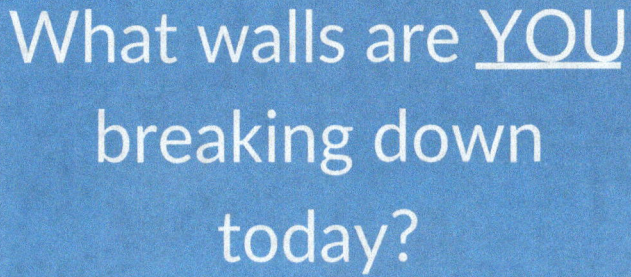

What walls are YOU breaking down today?

SET AN INTENTION

GIVE YOURSELF
A PEP TALK

THINK BIG

GO OUT &
MAKE IT
HAPPEN

With **YOU**

on my side

I can do **ANYTHING**

With **LOVE**

in my heart

I can do **EVERYTHING**

What are your
WILDEST DREAMS?

WHAT IS YOUR EVERYTHING?

LOVE YOUR SELF

Don't wait for someone else to give you what YOU can provide.

YOU DON'T NEED TO BE LIKE ANYONE ELSE

YOU ARE ONE-OF-A-KIND
YOU DO YOU, BOO!

WHAT MAKES YOU, YOU?
SHOW US WHO YOU ARE

AT TIMES OUR INNER VOICE CAN BE SO LOUD. BUT, IS THE CONVERSATION POSITIVE OR NEGATIVE?

YOU CONTROL THE DIALOGUE.

WHAT DO _YOU_ HEAR?
LIST 3 UPLIFTING INTENTIONS YOU CAN FOCUS ON

What appears when *YOU* replace doubt with *TRUST*?

What are you manifesting in your life?

LET YOUR SONG BE HEARD

THE MIND CAN BE AN ENSEMBLE OF THOUGHTS, A COLLECTION OF RHYTHMS THAT NEED TO BE EXPRESSED

What's on your playlist?

Relationships are currency

TRUST
LOVE
COMPASSION
RESPECT
LAUGHTER
JOY
KINDNESS
COMMITMENT

Invest fully and the dividends are priceless

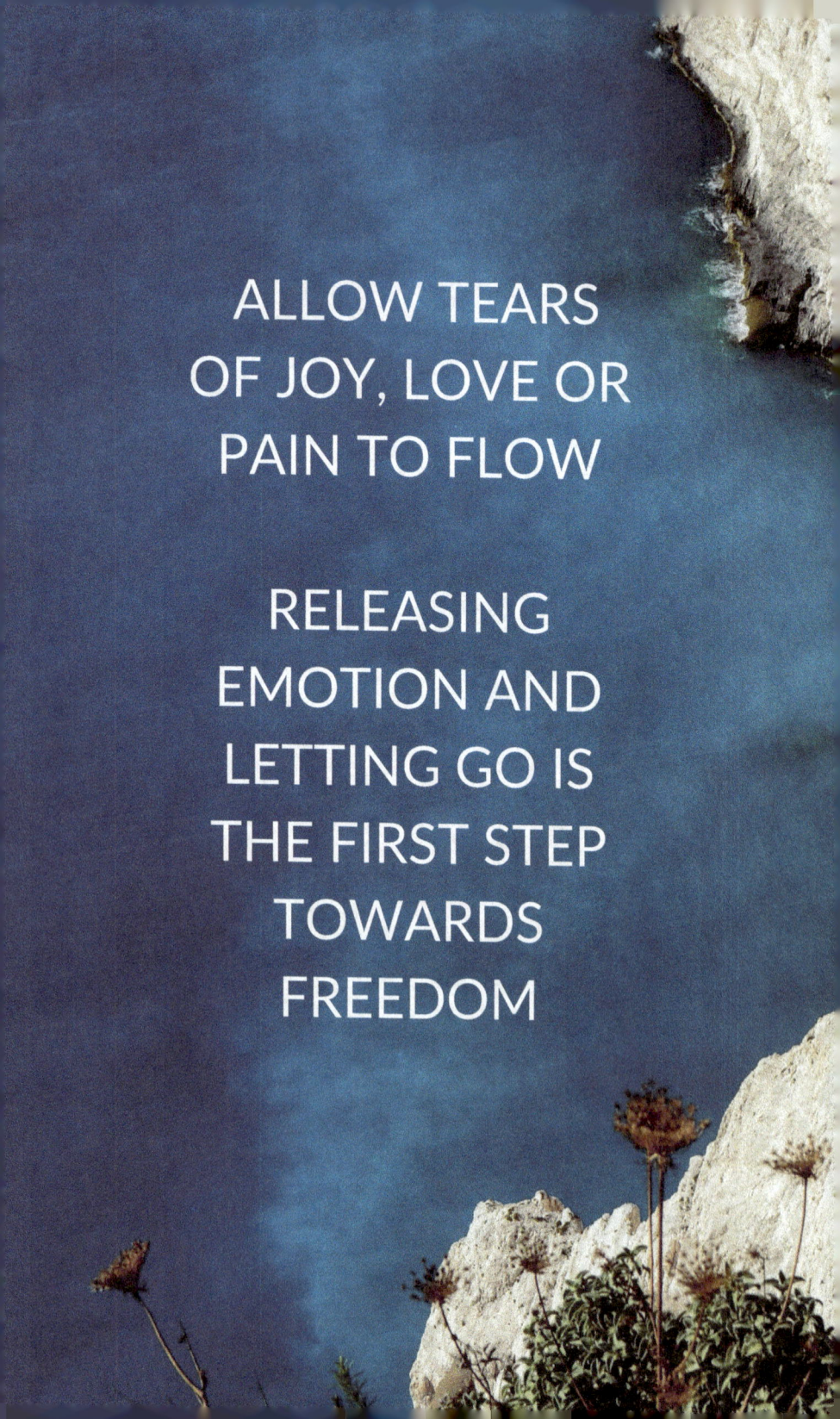

What do YOUR tears hold?

EACH NEW DAWN IS ANOTHER BLANK PAGE IN THE DIARY OF LIFE

YOUR IMAGINATION IS THE BEST TOOL FOR CREATING THE LIFE YOU WANT.

YOU ARE WHAT YOU BELIEVE.

As a child, what did your imagination reveal about YOU?

MANIFESTING IS MORE THAN A SINGLE THOUGHT. IT'S FOLLOWING FEELINGS WITH INTENTIONAL ACTIONS.

What actions will *you* take to manifest your dreams?

FOCUS. FEEL AND EMBRACE YOUR TRANSFORMATION.

WHAT AMAZING POSSIBILITIES CAN YOU IMAGINE FOR YOUR LIFE?

SOMETIMES YOU HAVE TO TAKE A STEP BACK IN ORDER TO MOVE FORWARD

BE PROUD.
FEEL THE
ACCOMPLISHMENT
OF
HOW FAR <u>YOU</u>
HAVE COME.

WHAT OBSTACLES HAVE <u>YOU</u> OVERCOME TO GET HERE?

Where do you find YOUR joy?

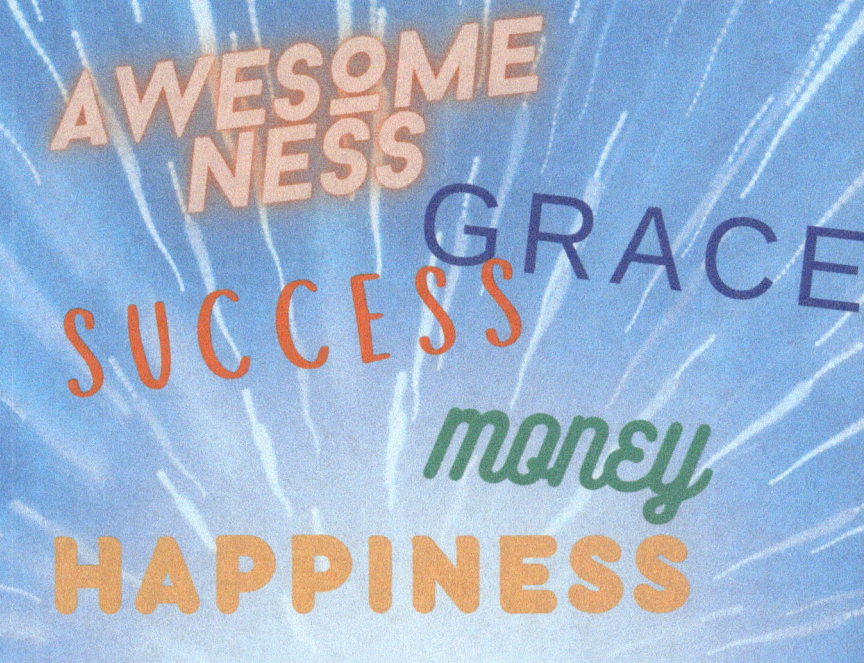

ACKNOWLEDGEMENTS

My two amazing children, Zakk and Audra, thank you for always lifting me up, you're my true heart and soul.

My mom, Lupe, thank you for your inspiration.

My aunt, Lita, thank you for your strength.

My stepmom, Dorothy, thank you for your unwavering support.

Kristine Bell - thank you for our friendship and for helping me make this happen.

Stacey Farish - thank you for unknowingly changing my life, a friendship cemented with laughs and wine.

Dana Perri - thank you for being a fantastic fitness coach who keeps me fit and pushes me to be my best...the ultimate SHIFT.

Anné Gangel - thank you for helping me unblock and tap into my intuitive gifts.

And finally to Heather, my muse, my love, but most importantly, my best friend. Thank you for believing in this crazy Gemini. I love you more than words can express.

SIGN UP FOR INFORMATION AND
UPDATES ON OUR TOOLS FOR
PURSUING HAPPINESS AND JOY
www.silverheartproductions.com/contact

www.ingramcontent.com/pod-product-compliance
Lightning Source LLC
LaVergne TN
LVHW022001060526
838201LV00048B/1649